W9-CAL-618

WOMEN IN
Television

BY XINA M. UHL

CONTENT CONSULTANT
Suzanne Leonard, PhD
Associate Professor
Simmons College

Core Library

Cover image: Zendaya was named Favorite TV Actress
at the 2017 Kids' Choice Awards.

An Imprint of Abdo Publishing
abdopublishing.com

abdopublishing.com

Published by Abdo Publishing, a division of ABDO, PO Box 398166,
Minneapolis, Minnesota 55439. Copyright © 2019 by Abdo Consulting
Group, Inc. International copyrights reserved in all countries. No part of this
book may be reproduced in any form without written permission from the
publisher. Core Library™ is a trademark and logo of Abdo Publishing.

Printed in the United States of America, North Mankato, Minnesota
042018
092018

 **THIS BOOK CONTAINS
RECYCLED MATERIALS**

Cover Photo: Frazer Harrison/KCA2017/Getty Images Entertainment/Getty Images
Interior Photos: Frazer Harrison/KCA2017/Getty Images Entertainment/Getty Images, 1; Evan
Agostini/Invision/AP Images, 4–5; Fox Broadcasting Co./Photofest, 7, 43; Arthur Mola/Invision/AP
images, 9; TVA/PictureGroup/Invision/Academy of Television Arts & Sciences/AP Images, 12–13;
AP Images, 15, 19, 45; Bettmann/Getty Images, 16; WB/Photofest, 20; Richard Shotwell/Invision/AP
Images, 22–23, 30; Red Line Editorial, 24, 34; John Shearer/Invision/AP Images, 26; NBC/Photofest,
29; Phil McCarten/Invision/Television Academy/AP Images, 32–33; Joe Scarnici/WireImage/Getty
Images, 37; Jordan Strauss/Invision/Television Academy/AP Images, 39

Editor: Marie Pearson
Imprint Designer: Maggie Villaume
Series Design Direction: Claire Vanden Branden

Library of Congress Control Number: 2017962806

Publisher's Cataloging-in-Publication Data

Names: Uhl, Xina M, author.
Title: Women in television / by Xina M. Uhl.
Description: Minneapolis, Minnesota : Abdo Publishing, 2019. | Series: Women in the arts |
        Includes online resources and index.
Identifiers: ISBN 9781532114786 (lib.bdg.) | ISBN 9781532154614 (ebook)
Subjects: LCSH: Female actors--Juvenile literature. | Women in television broadcasting--
        Juvenile literature. | Women in art--Juvenile literature. | Women in the performing
        arts--Juvenile literature.
Classification: DDC 791.4502--dc23

CONTENTS

Women Make Waves

Mindy Kaling stood on a pink and purple stage. She was at the Beverly Wilshire Hotel in Beverly Hills, California. She wore a stunning floor-length royal-blue dress. Her fellow cast members of *The Mindy Project* joined her on the stage. They had just received the 2016 Gracie Award for Outstanding Ensemble Cast in a Comedy. The Alliance for Women in Media awarded the first Gracies in 1975. The Gracie Awards are one way the group celebrates and supports women in the media industry.

Mindy Kaling has received several awards for her work.

Kaling's Family

Mindy Kaling was born and raised in Cambridge, Massachusetts. Her parents moved to the United States from India. Her mother is a doctor, which inspired *The Mindy Project*. In 1980, only 206,000 Indian immigrants lived in the United States. By 2015, that number had grown to nearly 2.4 million. American television features few Indian American actors. Kaling has been called a pioneer.

The audience listened and laughed at Mindy's acceptance speech. She didn't mince words: "For years and years, the role of a lead actress on a sitcom was to do two things: look amazing and make one-third of what my male co-star makes. I want to be clear. I do always look amazing on the show; and no man on that show makes more money than me."

Kaling rose to fame as one of the writers and actors on the popular comedy *The Office* (2005–2013). The show earned her six Emmy nominations from 2007 to 2011. The Emmys are the highest American award for

Kaling played a doctor in *The Mindy Project*.

television shows of all types. Her success also brought her to the attention of Fox Television.

There, she developed and starred in the romantic comedy *The Mindy Project* (2012–2017). Kaling played the main character. The show focuses on a doctor struggling with her love life. The sitcom was the first to star an Indian American. Reviewers really liked the show. They called it charming, off-beat, smart, and wildly funny. The show moved to Hulu, a streaming video service, in 2015. It ran for two more seasons before wrapping up.

Kaling has also performed in movies, with voice roles in *Wreck-It Ralph* and *Inside Out*. She's written several books about her life and has more than 10 million followers on Twitter.

Kaling hasn't finished with TV, though. She is the creator of the NBC comedy *Champions*. She also has plans to adapt the 1994 film *Four Weddings and a Funeral* into a Hulu series. Kaling is bringing it to TV as a writer and executive producer. Kaling is only one of many talented women in TV today.

Phyllis Smith, Amy Poehler, and Mindy Kaling, *left to right*, voiced the emotions Sadness, Joy, and Disgust in the film *Inside Out*.

WOMEN AND TV

As the twenty-first century unfolds, diverse women have taken on a greater role in the television industry. They appear behind the camera as well as in front of it. Actors are just one small part of a huge industry. This industry involves directors, writers, casting agents, set designers, makeup artists, video editors, and more. Men had most of these jobs in the past. But women are making their mark. Women have been involved in television from the beginning. Today, they are filling more roles on both sides of the camera.

STRAIGHT TO THE
SOURCE

Mindy Kaling has been involved in many different projects. In 2013, she spoke about her experience being interviewed about her work:

> More than half the questions I am asked are about the politics of the way I look. What it feels like to be not skinny/dark-skinned/a minority/not conventionally pretty/female/etc. It's not very interesting to me, but I know it's interesting to people reading an interview. Sometimes I get jealous of white male showrunners when 90 percent of their questions are about characters, story structure, creative inspiration, or . . . even the business of getting a show on the air. Because as a result the interview of me reads like I'm interested only in talking about my outward appearance and the politics of being a minority and how I fit into Hollywood, blah blah blah. I want to shout, "Those were the only questions they asked!"

Source: "Lena Dunham Interviewed Mindy Kaling, and It Was Glorious." *Huffington Post*. Huffington Post, November 12, 2013. Web. Accessed April 17, 2018.

What's the Big Idea?

Read the text carefully. What is the main idea? What examples does Kaling use to support her idea?

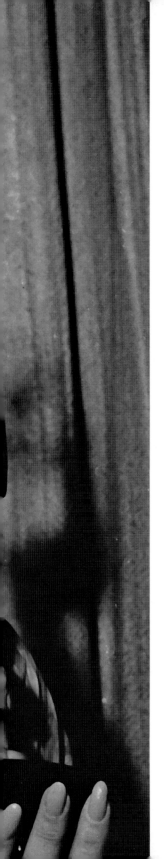

Making History

Television was invented in the 1930s. It didn't become popular until after World War II (1939–1945) ended. In 1948, roughly 2 percent of American households owned televisions. Less than ten years later, that number jumped to 70 percent. Early TV programming grew out of radio broadcasts. Popular programs included Westerns, mysteries, and variety shows. Another familiar format was the situation comedy, or sitcom. A sitcom tells a story about people who end up in funny situations.

One of the greatest sitcom stars in history was Lucille Ball. She became a TV pioneer with her comedy *I Love Lucy*. The show ran on CBS

Lucille Ball received an Emmy in 1967.

Breaking Taboos

I Love Lucy broke TV ground in more than one way. Lucy's husband on the show and in real life was Cuban Desi Arnaz. This was TV's first relationship between a white person and a person of color. At that time, there were restrictions about what could be shown on television. The couple's bedroom on the show had two twin beds, not one bed. The network became very nervous when Ball became pregnant. She was only the second woman on TV to appear pregnant. She wasn't allowed to use the word *pregnant* on the show. It was seen as too rude for the audience. Instead, Lucy said she was "expecting." But the episode in which her baby, Ricky, was born was one of the show's most popular.

from 1951 to 1957. It features married couple Lucy and Ricky Ricardo. They live in a Manhattan apartment. There, Lucy finds herself in silly situations of her own making. In one episode called "Job Switching," Lucy and her friend Ethel get jobs in a chocolate factory. They cannot keep up with the work. Instead, they eat the candy to hide their mistakes. *I Love Lucy* was one of the most popular shows of its time.

Vivian Vance, *left*, and Lucille Ball played Ethel and Lucy in *I Love Lucy*.

Ball had previously appeared in dozens of movies. She met and married Cuban bandleader Desi Arnaz in 1940. They formed the production

company Desilu Studios in 1950. Ball became the first woman in Hollywood to lead a production company. Desilu produced *I Love Lucy* and other shows. Arnaz played Ball's husband on *I Love Lucy*. Though the show ended in 1957, reruns continue to air more than 60 years later. *TV Guide* voted Ball the Greatest Star of All Time in 1996.

CHANGING TIMES

Many women had been employed in factories and stores during World War II. But during the 1950s, many women were encouraged to quit their jobs to stay home and raise a family. During the 1960s, women began to enter college and the workforce in greater numbers. TV shows reflected women's growing independence. Marlo Thomas starred in the comedy *That Girl* from 1966 to 1971. The show covers a single actress's adventures in New York. Thomas was the show's star and its producer. She was nominated for four Emmy Awards for her work.

Ted Russell and Marlo Thomas starred in *That Girl* from 1966 to 1971.

The Golden Girls

NBC's *The Golden Girls* ran from 1985 to 1992. The sitcom focuses on four senior women sharing a home in Florida. With wit and sarcasm, the actors knew how to deliver the lines just right. The subject matter touches on many important issues, too. Aging, marriage equality, racism, and physical disabilities are all tackled with humor. The heart of the show is the women's friendships with one another. The women show that friendships can endure many ups and downs. The show was nominated for 68 Emmys and won 11 times.

Thomas served as a role model for young women, and *That Girl* helped inspire future shows.

The Mary Tyler Moore Show was a hit in the 1970s. It was named after its female star. The show broke ground by focusing on character Mary Richards's career working in a newsroom. The show pushed boundaries by mentioning birth control, the wage gap,

Mary Tyler Moore, *left*, led her own TV show in which she starred as a news producer.

Buffy the Vampire Slayer featured a female action hero.

and other social issues. Mary Tyler Moore also formed her own production company, MTM Enterprises.

At the time, few women had management jobs in the entertainment industry. Women had been locked out of jobs as directors and writers. The government even investigated network hiring in the early 1970s.

In the 1980s and 1990s, TV shows increased the variety of female characters they included. Women's roles also increased behind the scenes in TV.

More women became producers and executives. As working women became more common in society, viewers wanted more shows with central female characters.

The types of female characters also changed over time. The show *Buffy the Vampire Slayer* ran from 1997–2003. The main character, Buffy, was a teenage girl who had special powers. She and her friends fought monsters while trying to deal with normal high school problems. *Buffy* was one of the first shows to focus on a female action hero. Its success paved the way for many popular shows today.

Further Evidence

Review this chapter to identify the main point. Name two pieces of evidence. Then read the article mentioned below. Find one quote that stands out to you. Does this new quote support an existing piece of evidence in the chapter or add a new one?

The Impact of The Mary Tyler Moore Show
abdocorelibrary.com/women-in-television

On the Screen

For a long time, TVs only had a few channels. Eventually, cable and satellite TV offered more options. Starting in the early 2000s, online video services became popular. Sites such as YouTube, Netflix, and Hulu began creating their own shows. These new options have provided more opportunities for women to play more roles.

As online drama continues to grow, web series are reaching new heights. *The Lizzie Bennet Diaries* is a modern adaptation of Jane Austen's 1813 novel *Pride and Prejudice*. The show is set up as a series of video diaries. In 2013, it was the first web series to win an Emmy. The producer, Jenni Powell, has

Ashley Clements starred in *The Lizzie Bennet Diaries*.

FEMALE LEADS IN BROADCAST TELEVISION

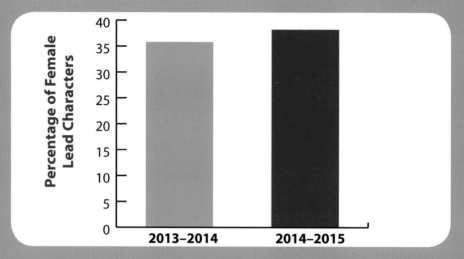

The number of women in television varies by category. In broadcast television, 35.8 percent of shows had female lead characters in the 2013–14 season. That number increased to 38.2 percent for 2014–15. The numbers still don't reflect the real world. Women were 50.8 percent of the US population in 2010. Why do you think there aren't more women leads? Think about the shows you watch. Do they have female leads?

created other online adaptations as well. Her latest work is a series based on *Peter Pan*. It's called *The New Adventures of Peter and Wendy*.

Traditional networks and online video services sometimes interact. Network executives pay attention to YouTube channels with large followings, which can result in TV careers. It can also work in the other direction. Some TV stars create their own work online.

ZENDAYA

Zendaya Coleman was born in Oakland, California, in 1996 to an African American father and a white mother. She started acting and dancing when she was a young child. She modeled for Macy's and Old Navy and danced in a Sears commercial. She shortened her stage name to "Zendaya." At age 14, she entered the spotlight when she starred in Disney Channel's *Shake It Up*. From 2015 to 2018, she appeared as spy K. C. Cooper in Disney's *K. C. Undercover*. In 2017, she was in the film *Spider-Man: Homecoming*.

TINA FEY

Tina Fey got her start in Chicago, Illinois, with the Second City comedy group. In 1997, she joined the TV comedy show *Saturday Night Live* as one of the few female writers. She became the show's first female head writer in 1999. She made another career switch

in 2000 when she began performing on the show.

From there, Fey's star kept rising. She adapted the popular book *Mean Girls* into a movie in 2004. She played a teacher in the film. She then created her own sitcom, *30 Rock*, which she wrote and starred in from 2006 to 2013. Since the end of *30 Rock*, Fey cocreated the Netflix series *Unbreakable Kimmy Schmidt*. She is

Writing to Inspire

Actress and producer Reese Witherspoon credited Tina Fey with inspiring her to help women in entertainment. Fey's 2011 memoir *Bossypants* says that women in comedy are often called "crazy." The remedy for that, Fey says, is for more women to become producers and executives. Witherspoon told Fox News, "I hope to . . . create opportunities for other women to tell their stories, because women aren't just girlfriends and wives, you know, in movies, to big leading men. Those are great roles, but I feel like women are much more complex than that."

Tina Fey, *left*, and Amy Poehler have worked together on many projects.

a vocal advocate for women in the television industry.

AMY POEHLER

Fey often pairs up with another *Saturday Night Live* veteran, Amy Poehler. Poehler started out on *Saturday Night Live* in 2001. She made her name acting, writing, and producing the sitcom *Parks and Recreation*

(2009–2015). *Time* magazine named her on its 2011 list of the 100 most influential people.

Rashida Jones, *left*, and Amy Poehler starred on *Parks and Recreation*, a comedy about city workers.

Issa Rae's show *Insecure* premiered on HBO in 2016.

ISSA RAE

Issa Rae is an African American actor, writer, director, and producer. She created the hit web series *The Misadventures of Awkward Black Girl*. The show had more than 300,000 YouTube subscribers and

23 million views by 2018. She appeared on *Glamour* magazine's "35 Under 35" list and *Entertainment Weekly*'s "Breaking Big" list. The success of the show brought her to the attention of HBO. HBO encouraged her to write a similar character for a show on its network. Rae created and stars in the comedy show *Insecure*. She plays a woman trying to juggle work, friends, family, and a complicated love life. *Insecure* received a Golden Globe nomination in 2016.

Explore Online

What is the main point of the chapter? What details support the point? Go to the article about YouTube stars at the website below. Find a quote to support or disagree with the main point.

YouTube Stars
abdocorelibrary.com/women-in-television

CHAPTER
FOUR

Behind the Scenes

Many people work behind the scenes to produce a TV show. In a comedy, for example, writers produce funny scripts about the lives of fictional characters. Writers create dialogue. They envision where the story takes place and what happens in it. Location managers find places to film. They make sure that locations outside of the studio will have what the show needs and be ready for actors. Set designers and costume designers are responsible for the look of the show. Directors work to bring scripts to life,

Shonda Rhimes was named to the Television Academy Hall of Fame in 2017.

FEMALE CREATORS MEAN MORE FEMALE WRITERS

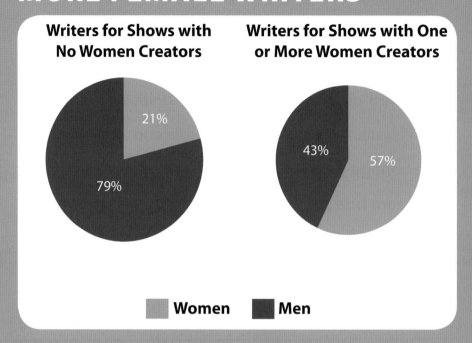

Writers for Shows with No Women Creators

21%

79%

Writers for Shows with One or More Women Creators

43%

57%

Women   Men

The charts above demonstrate how a TV show's writing staff changes when women are present in leadership roles. When one or more women are in these roles, the number of female writers hired rises sharply. Do you think having more female writers changes what kinds of stories are told? What other differences might happen?

pulling together the actors, writers, camera operators, and creators.

SHONDA RHIMES

Shonda Rhimes is a powerhouse in TV today. A showrunner, she got her start in film. After writing screenplays for films such as *Crossroads* (2002), she moved into TV. She is known for a practice called "color-blind casting" where she does not specify the race or ethnicity of her characters. As a result, her casts are some of the most diverse on contemporary television. She first used this technique for the popular medical drama *Grey's Anatomy*. The show began in 2005 and features doctors and patients of all races. Diverse casts appear in Rhimes's other shows as well.

Scandal, a political drama, ran from 2012 to 2018 on ABC. *How to Get Away with Murder* began in 2014

In Charge

Women lead a variety of shows, ranging from cartoons to historical dramas. Charlotte Fullerton was story editor or writer for *Ben 10*, *My Little Pony*, and *Kim Possible*. Ryan Case won an Emmy for her editing work on ABC's *Modern Family*. LaToya Morgan received two NAACP Image Award nominations for her writing on *Turn: Washington's Spies*. Lauren Faust has worked as producer for *My Little Pony* and director for *The Powerpuff Girls*. She works with Cartoon Network, Warner Brothers, Hasbro, and Disney.

on ABC. It features the legal system and law-school life, along with crime stories. Rhimes's shows have different topics, but they also have things in common. They have hardworking female characters, intense settings, and romantic plots.

Each of Rhimes's shows is produced by her company, Shondaland. The shows have won many awards, including eight Emmys. In 2017, Rhimes left ABC. She signed a deal to produce multiple projects with the streaming service Netflix.

JANE ESPENSON

TV writer and producer Jane Espenson is well known as a science-fiction writer. She has won two Hugo Awards for television. The Hugos are given to the best sci-fi or fantasy stories of the year. Born in Ames, Iowa, she spent her youth watching lots of television. She attended college at the University of California, Berkeley. While there, she wrote a script for *Star Trek: The Next Generation*. The script helped her

Jane Espenson

Jane Espenson has written episodes for many sci-fi shows.

land her first writing job on *Buffy the Vampire Slayer*. In 2003, she won a Hugo Award for the Buffy episode "Conversations with Dead People." She won another Hugo Award in 2012 for her work on *Game of Thrones.* Espenson's other television credits include *Gilmore Girls, Warehouse 13, The Inside, Tru Calling, Battlestar*

Galactica, and *Once Upon a Time*. She teamed with Brad Bell to create the comedy *Husbands* (2011–2013). The web series is about a gay couple adapting to married life.

CREW MEMBERS

Crew members have many different duties. They may be makeup artists or sound engineers. Some compose music or build sets. Others design costumes or

Doctor Who

The British Broadcasting Corporation (BBC) show *Doctor Who* started in 1963. It ended in 1989 but came back in 2005. An alien called the Doctor travels throughout time and space. The first producer, Verity Lambert, was the BBC's only female producer at the time. Though this was her first production job, she quickly proved her talents. Many other women have been involved in *Doctor Who* behind the scenes. Delia Derbyshire arranged the original theme music. Julie Gardner was executive producer from 2005 to 2010. Rachel Talalay directed the 2017 season finale.

Sound editing is just one of many behind-the-scenes jobs. Ginger Geary is the award-winning sound editor for Netflix drama series *Stranger Things*.

assist directors. They may work in postproduction special effects. They may edit video. There are dozens of different roles, from camera operation to managing lighting. Women have had a difficult time getting into this job market—at least in the past.

The TV industry continues to change as time goes on and technology upgrades. Trends make it clear that the TV industry is healthy and strong. Women's roles will continue to grow. There is still plenty of room for improvement, but there's hope for the future.

STRAIGHT TO THE
SOURCE

Caroline Stack has worked in postproduction for shows such as *Falling Skies* (2011–2015) and *Wayward Pines* (2016). She says of the career:

> When I first entered the business as a graphics coordinator in 2006 I was the only woman out of ten people in my post-production department. From what I've observed, more women have entered the field since then, and there's more diversity as well. . . . I love my job because I get to hang out with creative and talented people who are amazing to work with. . . . If you have the motivation of just wanting to tell stories—motivation that comes from inside you—you'll do well. People who enter the business for celebrity or fame don't do as well.

> Source: Caroline Stack. E-mail interview. 13 November 2017.

Consider Your Audience

Adapt this passage for a different audience, such as your principal or friends. Write a blog post conveying this same information for the new audience. How does your post differ from the original text and why?

NOTABLE
WORKS

The Mindy Project starring Mindy Kaling

A romantic comedy television series about Doctor Mindy Lahiri, an OBGYN who is great helping her patients through pregnancy but not so great at love. Her quirky coworkers help her figure out her priorities.

I Love Lucy starring Lucille Ball

A black and white, Emmy-winning sitcom about a zany and determined wife and mother who often schemes up hilarious ways to make it big in show business.

Grey's Anatomy produced by Shonda Rhimes

A medical drama that follows Meredith Grey and fellow doctors and nurses at Seattle Grace Hospital.

Shake It Up starring Zendaya

A Disney Channel show that focuses on two high school girls, CeCe Jones and Rocky Blue, who find work as backup dancers on a local television show.

STOP AND
THINK

Say What?

Learning about the TV industry and its many jobs means reading a lot of new vocabulary. Find five terms you are not familiar with. Use a dictionary to define them. Then, write the meanings in your own words. Use each new term in a sentence.

Tell the Tale

Chapter Two talks about the history of women in TV. Imagine you want to create a show about women today. What kinds of stories would you tell? What jobs would the women in the show have?

Surprise Me

Chapter Four talks about female TV crew members. After reading the book, what two or three facts about women who work behind the scenes surprised you? Write a few sentences explaining why you found each fact surprising.

Another View

This book covers the roles women have played in front of the camera and behind it. Ask an adult to help you research what it takes to be an actor, writer, director, or crew member in today's world. Write a short essay comparing and contrasting the new source's point of view with that of this book's author. How does each author approach the subject? Are the sources similar? Are they different? Why?

GLOSSARY

adaptation
a movie or TV show based on a book

diverse
including different races, ethnicities, genders, sexualities, ages, and classes

lead
the main character in a television series

network
a television company that makes shows and airs them on TV

postproduction
work, such as adjusting sound and adding visual effects, that occurs after video has been shot

producer
the person in charge of a show

production company
a company that funds the creation of television programs

showrunner
the person who has creative authority and management responsibility for a television program

sitcom
a humorous show with the same cast of characters from episode to episode

web series
a TV show that is created and released on the Internet

ONLINE RESOURCES

To learn more about women in television, visit our free resource websites below.

Visit **abdocorelibrary.com** for free Common Core resources for teachers and students, including vetted activities, multimedia, and booklinks, for deeper subject comprehension.

Visit **abdobooklinks.com** for free additional online weblinks for further learning. These links are routinely monitored and updated to provide the most current information available.

LEARN MORE

Lajiness, Katie. *Zendaya*. Minneapolis, MN: Abdo, 2018.

Pollack, Pam. *Who Was Lucille Ball?* New York, NY: Grosset and Dunlap, 2017.

INDEX

About the Author

Xina M. Uhl has written more than 20 books for young people. One of her favorite subjects is women's history and accomplishments. When she isn't reading or writing, she can be found traveling, hiking, or playing with her dogs.